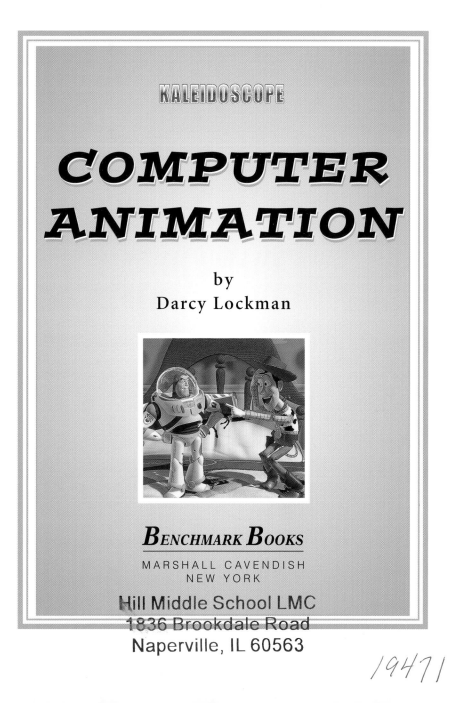

KALEIDOSCOPE

COMPUTER ANIMATION

by
Darcy Lockman

Benchmark Books

MARSHALL CAVENDISH
NEW YORK

Series Consultant:
Dr. Paul Benjamin
School of Computer Science and Information Systems
Pace University

Benchmark Books
Marshall Cavendish Corporation
99 White Plains Road
Tarrytown, NY 10591

Library of Congress Cataloging-in-Publication Data
Lockman, Darcy, date
Computer animation / by Darcy Lockman.
p. cm. — (Kaleidoscope)
Included bibliographical references and index.
Summary: Explains how computer animation is used to make entire films, indicates how it differs from traditional animation, and includes information on the development of that technology.
ISBN 0-7614-1048-1
1. Computer animation-Juvenile literature. [1. Computer animation.] I. Title. II. Kaleidoscope (Tarrytown, NY)
TR897.7   L63   2000
778.5'34-dc21   99-058310

Photo research by Candlepants, Inc.
Cover Photo: Photofest © The Walt Disney Company
Photo credits: 5, Photofest © Twentieth Century Fox; 6, Photofest © The Walt Disney Company; 8, Photofest © The Walt Disney Company; 10, Photo Researchers, James Kind-Holmes/Science Photo Library; 12, Corbis-Bettmann, Digital Art; 14, Photofest; 16, Photofest; 18, Photofest, John Shannon; 20, Corbis-Bettmann; 22, Photofest; Corbis-Bettmann, Roger Ressmeyer; 26, Image Bank, A.T. Willett; 29, Photofest; 30, Corbis-Bettmann, Dan Lamont; 33, Corbis, Roger Ressmeyer; 34, Corbis, Roger Ressmeyer; 38, Photofest; 40, Corbis-Bettmann, David H. Wells; 42, Photofest, © Lucasfilm LTD.

Diagram on page 37 by Gysela Pacheco

Printed in Italy

6 5 4 3 2 1

CONTENTS

ABOUT COMPUTER ANIMATION

Computers are everywhere—in schools and businesses, homes and stores. You've probably seen movies and television shows, or played video games that have been created with the help of computers. People in film and television use computers, and their imaginations, to do everything from creating cool opening credits to making special effects appear more realistic. They even make entire films using computers. All of this is done with *computer animation*. This is an interesting process. Let's take a look.

4

The movie Independence Day *used computer animation to make its special effects look more realistic.*

A cell from a traditionally animated film by Walt Disney. This cell was drawn and colored in by hand.

A NEW WAY TO ANIMATE

Traditional *animation* is created from a series of drawings. These drawings are hand-drawn with pencil and paper and colored ink. When they are filmed in order and then quickly played back, they look as though they are moving. You may have seen a *flip book,* a small book with a picture on each page. Each picture is slightly different. When flipped with your thumb, the pictures look like they are moving. Cartoons work the same way. When you see a cartoon character—like Donald Duck or Pinocchio—move on film, what you're really seeing is a group of different pictures passing very quickly before a camera.

Cartoons are still created this way. But today animators can use computers to make animated films. Computer *software* allows animation artists to create their drawings on the computer. It does other things, too. It can be used to move those drawings, to light a

A scene from A Bug's Life. *This movie was computer animated. Instead of drawing each cell by hand, the animators created the characters and background on their computers.*

scene, to give drawings colors and textures, and to record the final film. If you've seen movies like *Toy Story* or *A Bug's Life,* you've seen computer animation in action.

COMPUTER ANIMATION PAST AND PRESENT

The technology that allows pictures, and not just words and numbers, to appear on a computer screen is called *computer graphics technology.* It was developed in the early 1950s. At first, like a lot of new technology, it was only used by the military and scientists. The air force used it to train fighter pilots. Electrical engineers used it to test equipment. None of the early computer graphics systems, though, were applied to artwork.

Computer animation is still used to help train pilots. Here, a pilot trains to fly a Boeing 737-300 airliner.

During the 1970s and 1980s, computers became more common, and things began to change. This was mostly because artists became interested in trying out the technology for themselves. They took the computer graphics technology that scientists had been using and started using it to create art.

This image was created completely on computer. Artists first experimented with computers in the late 1970s.

13

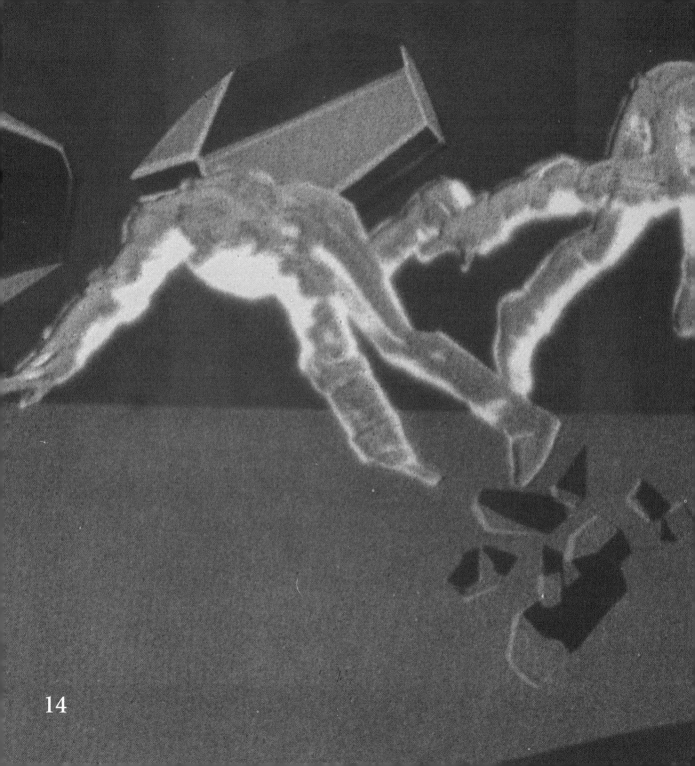

14

They loved what they could do. Then, in 1982, computer graphics technology went mainstream. It was used in a movie, *Tron*. The story of a man who gets lost in a video game, *Tron* had over twenty minutes of computer animation. Soon after *Tron* and throughout the 1980s, computer animation began to be used on television as well, in everything from commercials to videos.

A scene from Tron, *the first movie to use computer animation.*

15

Today, animators use computers in many different ways. They can create lifelike dinosaurs, as they did for *Jurassic Park*. They can transform the shape and colors of faces, as they did in *Terminator 2: Judgement Day*. They can create Coca-Cola drinking polar bears, or talking M&Ms. Just about anything the mind can imagine, animators can create with computer animation software.

Terminator II, Judgment Day *came out just over ten years after* Tron, *in the early 1990s. The special effects were much more exciting.*

17

PANAVISION

PLATINUM

1000   S245·006·0211·20   Roll   52
M#2   'ALWAYS'   6. ·89

2

18   A

Creating an animated film is a lot like creating a film with real people and places. As with *live-action* films, animated films follow three basic steps: preproduction, production, and postproduction. Can you guess what happens during these stages?

In a live-action movie, the filming takes place during production. Here, director Steven Spielberg checks a scene.

19

Preproduction includes everything that happens before the film is actually made. It involves a lot of planning. The first step is writing a good *screenplay.* The screenplay tells a story through description, action, and *dialogue.*

Before any computer animation is done, the movie must be planned out. Here, an animator and an executive at Pixar Studios (creators of A Bug's Life *and the* Toy Story *movies) talk about their next project.*

SHANG! GET DOWN!

22

Once the screenplay is done, animators make it into a *storyboard.* A storyboard looks a little like a big comic book. Each drawing stands for a different *shot*—or moment of action—in the film. A storyboard is made up of hundreds or even thousands of drawings and shows everything that's going to happen in the film.

Chris Sanders, head of story and screenwriter for Disney's Mulan. *Behind him is the story-board for a scene from the movie.*

The film is actually made during the *production* stage. The first step is to create the characters, objects, and scenes described in the screenplay. These are created on the computer using software, or computer programs, created especially for animation (more on how this works later).

During production, characters are created on the computer. Here, an animator maps out a figure. Later, he will add color and texture to make the figure look real.

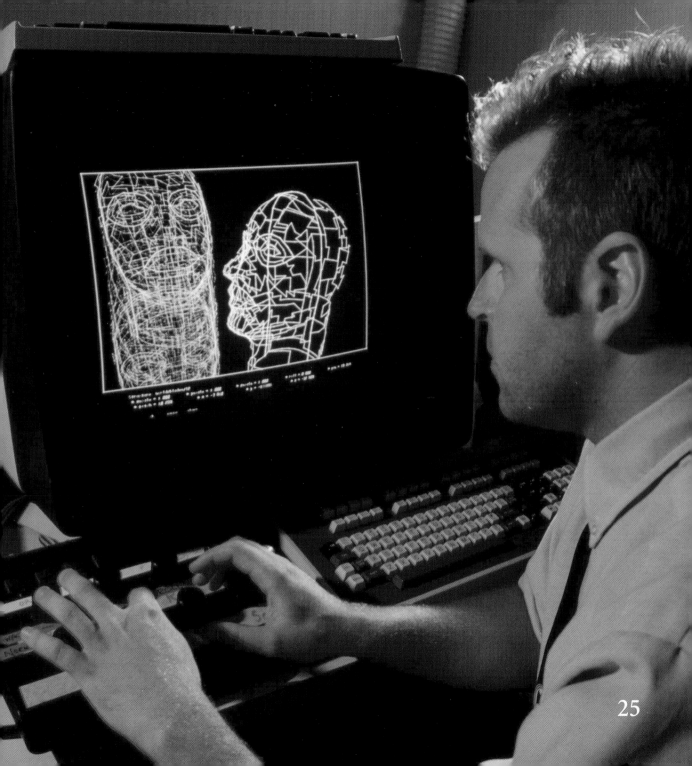

Once the characters, objects, and scenes are input, they can be arranged on the screen and animated with many different techniques. During production, the software records the film, much as your VCR at home records a TV show, so people can watch it over and over.

In the final step of production, the movie is recorded to film so that it can be played in a movie theater. Shown are three film-strips.

Postproduction, as you probably guessed, is what happens after production. During this stage, the final touches are put on an animated work. Music can be added, and mistakes in color, texture, and action can be corrected. Using computer animation software, animators can also add live images to their work. This means that they can make it look as if real people are moving inside the cartoon or talking to the animated characters.

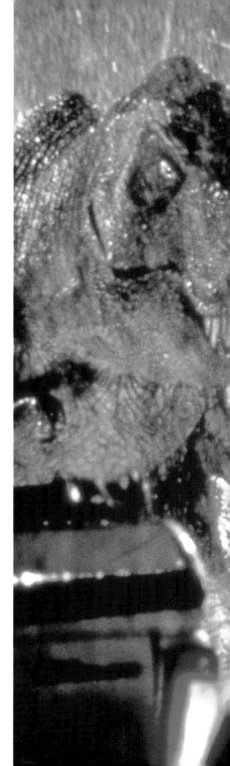

This scene from Jurassic Park *was filmed without the dinosaur. The actors had to pretend it was there. During postproduction, the dinosaur was added.*

MAKING THE MOVIE

Now that you know the three stages, let's look at production more closely. There are several different ways animators can create by computer. They may draw by hand, and then scan their drawings into the computer. They may also draw on a *digital pad,* which will put their drawings on the computer right away.

An image or, as here, a face can be scanned into the computer and then changed and moved by the animator.

31

Animators may also create using the computer alone. Have you ever done a connect the dots drawing? Drawing on the computer is something like that. The animator arranges the "dots," which the computer connects to make a character, object, or scene.

Once the drawing is on the computer, the animator can make it move by simply giving the computer commands. Creating characters, objects, and scenes this way is called *modeling*. All of this is done with computer software created just for computer animation.

Once drawn, the animator can move the figures by giving the computer commands.

When it comes time to color in a figure, anima-tors may select from a rainbow of hues.

After modeling, the scene needs to be filled in. This step is called *rendering.* Rendering is a little like coloring. During this phase, animators use the animation software to color frogs green or the sky blue. They can also add texture, which will make a tree trunk look rough, or a stuffed animal look fuzzy. Animators can also introduce light. They can make a ray of light spotlight a character or create shadows around things. All of these techniques help to make computer-generated images look more realistic.

Computer animation software also comes with a built-in camera. This isn't a camera like the one you would use to take pictures at a birthday party or the kind people use to take videos. Instead, this camera is like an eye that can look at a scene from many different angles. Try standing in a few different spots in your room. Do you see different things from each spot? Do the things in your room look different each time you move? Animators can look around a scene in much the same way using this camera. They can also use it to look at a scene up close or far away. This helps them decide which view of the scene they want to use in the movie.

This scene was created in a 3-D application. The artist used her software much in the same way a computer animator does to show different views of the scene.

View 1

View 2

View 3

View 4

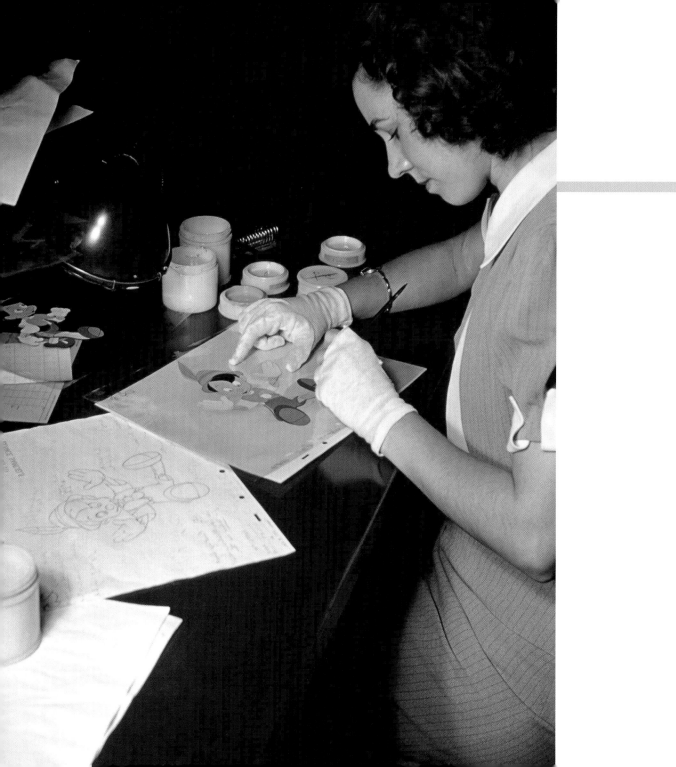

THE COMPUTER ANIMATION EDGE

Computer animation offers a lot of advantages over traditional animation. One is that it cuts down on some of the steps involved. This is especially true when it comes to making an animated character move. If Mickey Mouse is walking, for example, traditional animation would require a different drawing for each of the tiniest movements he needs to make. To get from one spot to the next could take up to eighty drawings!

Traditional animation requires hundreds of drawings for just one scene. Here, a woman works on Pinocchio. *She will have to do many more of these.*

With computer animation software, though, an animator can use a technique called *interpolation.* The computer itself can create the pictures in between Mickey's first and last movements by itself. It can do this much faster than a human can. That saves an animator a lot of time and energy.

Interpolation moves computer-animated figures from one place to the next.

41

When computers were first invented, all those years ago, no one ever dreamed that they would eventually have such an effect on movie making. Today, artists know they can rely on it to create magical scenes and stories. Many advances throughout the years have changed the programs we see on

Computer animation will continue to make movies better—just as it did for Star Wars Episode I: The Phantom Menace.

television and the films we see at the movies. Nobody knows how computer animation will transform entertainment in the future. But it will be fun to sit back and watch. Maybe one day you can even be a part of it yourself.

Animation   movement expressed through a series of drawings.

Computer animation   animation done on a computer.

Computer graphics technology   the technology that allows pictures, and not just words and numbers, to appear on a computer screen.

Dialogue   the part of a screenplay in which the character's words are written for the actor to read.

Digital Pad   an electronic pad. When animators draw on this, their drawing appears on the computer screen.

Flip book   a small book whose pages you flip to create the look of a short movie.

Interpolation   the technique by which a computer makes a computer-animated figure move.

Live-action   a film that uses real people, places, and things.

Modeling   creating the three-dimensional figures for an animated film on a computer.

Postproduction   the time after a film is shot, during

which finishing touches, like music and color, are added to a film.

Preproduction   the time before the actual shooting of a film, during which plans are made.

Production   the time during which an animated movie is actually created. This includes the drawing of the characters, scenes, and objects that will be in the movie.

Rendering   filling out an animated object with color, light, and texture.

Screenplay   the dialogue and shooting directions for a motion picture.

Shot   a single scene in a motion picture, filmed by one camera without a break.

Software   discs that contain the information a computer needs to do certain jobs.

Storyboard   the series of pictures that map out what will happen in an animated film.

FIND OUT MORE

Books:

Baker, Christopher. *Let There Be Light! Animating with the Computer.* New York, NY: Walker and Company, 1997.

Jortberg, Charles A. *Virtual Reality and Beyond.* Kids and Computers series. Minneapolis, MN: ABDO Publishing Company.

Steinhauser, Peggy L. *Mousetracks: A Kid's Computer Idea Book.* Berkley, CA: Tricycle Press, 1997.

Websites:

Nova: All About Special Effects:
http://www.pbs.org/wgbh/nova/specialfx/sfxhome.html

Pixar Animation Studios (Toy Story, etc.):
http://www.pixar.com

Shockwave Toys (computer animation games):
http://www.wayoutthere.com/shockwave/index.html

AUTHOR'S BIO

Darcy Lockman is a freelance writer who has written on technology for a number of young adult publications. She lives in New York City.

INDEX

Page numbers for illustrations are in boldface.